U.S. GOVERNMENT AGENCIES

WHAT DOES THE FDA DO?

DANIELLE HAYNES

PowerKiDS press

Published in 2026 by The Rosen Publishing Group, Inc.
2544 Clinton Street, Buffalo, NY 14224

First Edition

Editor: Danielle Haynes
Book Design: Rachel Rising

Photo Credits: Cover, p. 1 Dan Kosmayer/Shutterstock.com; Cover, pp. 5, 7, 8, 13 ,14 https://commons.wikimedia.org/wiki/File:Food_and_Drug_Administration_icon_2016.svg; Cover, pp. 1, 3-24 Madan Designer/Shutterstock.com; Cover, p. 1, 3-24 Art Posting/Shutterstock.com; p. 4 Fox_Ana/Shutterstock.com; p. 5 Tada Images/Shutterstock.com; p. 6 Drozd Irina/Shutterstock.com; p. 7 https://commons.wikimedia.org/wiki/File:%22Chamber_of_horrors.%22_Washington,_D.C.,_Dec._20._When_members_of_Congress_introduce_bills_on_new_drug_and_food_legislation_they_often_request_the_aid_of_Miss_Ruth_Lamb,_Chief_of_Public_LCCN2016872582.jpg; p. 9 https://commons.wikimedia.org/wiki/File:FDA_History_-_Sure_Cure_Cartoon.jpg; p. 10 https://commons.wikimedia.org/wiki/File:Flag_of_the_United_States_Department_of_Health_and_Human_Services.svg; p. 11 https://en.wikipedia.org/wiki/File:Robert_F._Kennedy_Jr.,_official_portrait_(2025)_(cropped_3-4).jpg; p. 11 https://commons.wikimedia.org/wiki/File:ActingCommissionerSaraBrenner.jpg; p. 12 BearFotos/Shutterstock.com; p. 13 Rix Pix Photography/Shutterstock.com; p. 15 Studio Romantic/Shutterstock.com; p. 16 everything possible/Shutterstock.com; p. 17 Jasen Wright/Shutterstock.com; p. 18 Billion Photos/Shutterstock.com; p. 19 KomootP/Shutterstock.com; pp. 20, 21 Gorodenkoff/Shutterstock.com.

Cataloging-in-Publication Data

Names: Haynes, Danielle.
Title: What does the FDA do? / Danielle Haynes.
Description: Buffalo, New York : PowerKids Press, 2026. | Series: U.S. government agencies | Includes glossary and index.
Identifiers: ISBN 9781499453119 (pbk.) | ISBN 9781499453126 (library bound) | ISBN 9781499453133 (ebook)
Subjects: LCSH: United States. Food and Drug Administration–Juvenile literature. | Food adulteration and inspection–United States–Juvenile literature.
Classification: LCC HD9000.9.U5 H38 2026 | DDC 363.192'0973–dc23

Manufactured in the United States of America

CPSIA Compliance Information: Batch #CSPK26. For Further Information contact Rosen Publishing at 1-800-237-9932.

CONTENTS

WHAT IS THE FDA?

Every day, people all over the United States eat food from the grocery store, take medicine from the **pharmacy**, and use makeup and hair products. But how do we know the things we're consuming and putting on our bodies are safe for us?

That's where the Food and Drug Administration (FDA) steps in! This is a U.S. government agency that protects public health. The FDA makes sure the food we eat is safe and the medicines we take won't make us feel worse. The agency even plays an important role in the creation of vaccines, such as the ones to limit the spread of COVID-19.

AGENCY INSIGHTS

The rules the U.S. government puts in place to keep food and drugs safe are also called regulations.

The FDA's headquarters is in Silver Spring, Maryland, just north of the capital of Washington, D.C.

FOOD AND DRUG SAFETY

Before the creation of the FDA, Americans had no way of knowing what was really in the packaged foods and medicines they consumed. Labels on such products could be **deceptive**. And dangerous things could be in them, including alcohol and other illegal drugs.

Around this time, a product called Othine promised to lighten freckles, but contained mercury, a dangerous chemical. Another, called Lash Lure, darkened eyebrows and eyelashes, but was so toxic it could cause blindness. Packaging was also deceptive, making it look like there was more product inside than there really was.

AGENCY INSIGHTS

In addition to food and medicines for humans, the FDA regulates products for pets and livestock animals.

Ruth Lamb, shown here in a photograph from 1937, was the FDA's first Chief Educational Officer. Lamb set up a "chamber of horrors" at the FDA that included products that were deceptive to the American public.

BIRTH OF THE FDA

The FDA has existed with its current name since July 1930, but there have been government employees working in food and drug safety since 1862. At that time, only a single scientist working in the U.S. Department of Agriculture (USDA) was studying the safety of agricultural products.

In 1906, the U.S. Congress passed the Pure Food and Drugs Act, which tasked the Bureau of Chemistry with doing this work. Harvey Wiley encouraged the passage of the act and was the country's first commissioner, or head, of food and drugs. In 1930, the agency was renamed the FDA. As of early 2025, more than 18,000 people work for the agency all over the country!

FDA

AGENCY INSIGHTS

A book by Upton Sinclair called *The Jungle*, which exposed the dirty conditions in the meat industry, was instrumental in the passage of the 1906 Pure Food and Drugs Act.

This political cartoon celebrates Commissioner of Food and Drugs Harvey Wiley for his work in food and drug safety.

HEALTH AND HUMAN SERVICES

Today, the FDA no longer is part of the USDA but instead is under the Department of Health and Human Services (HHS). These larger departments are 2 of 15 **cabinet**-level agencies that operate under the president of the United States. The heads of these departments are known as secretaries, which are appointed by the president and approved by the U.S. Senate.

In early 2025, President Donald Trump named Robert F. Kennedy Jr. as HHS secretary and Sara Brenner as commissioner of the FDA. The FDA commissioner answers to the HHS secretary.

Sara Brenner, left, worked as a public health physician in the FDA before becoming commissioner, and Robert F. Kennedy Jr. was an environmental lawyer before joining the cabinet.

FOOD SAFETY

The FDA has three main goals when it comes to food safety. First, it works to help Americans eat a **nutritious** diet to live long, healthy lives. The agency does this by encouraging the food industry to make more nutritious foods. For example, the FDA supports lowering salt in prepared foods and requires nutrition labels on packaging.

Second, the FDA works to improve food chemical safety. Potentially dangerous chemicals can enter our food supply through farming, processing, and packaging. FDA regulations make sure farms grow food in a safe environment and food manufacturers don't introduce unsafe chemicals. The agency also monitors chemicals in dietary supplements.

AGENCY INSIGHTS

Dietary supplements include things such as **vitamins** and **minerals**.

The FDA requires that most prepared foods include labels that list ingredients and nutrition values.

FOODBORNE ILLNESS

The third goal of the FDA is to prevent foodborne illnesses, also known as food poisoning. Many different bacteria and **pathogens** can cause foodborne illnesses. Some of the more common ones we hear about are e. coli, listeria, salmonella, and parasites. These can cause a variety of **symptoms**, including throwing up, stomach pain, headache, fever, and dizziness. Thousands of Americans die from foodborne illnesses each year.

The FDA researches ways to prevent these **contaminants** from being introduced to food. It also alerts the public when food products have been found to be contaminated. These alerts are called food recalls.

FDA

AGENCY INSIGHTS

During a food recall, grocery stores will remove the contaminated products from shelves. Consumers are also asked to throw out the food or return it to the store.

If a doctor finds you have a foodborne illness, they'll collect information about what you've eaten so they can track down where the contaminant came from.

DRUG SAFETY

In addition to food safety, the FDA plays an important role in approving and regulating medicinal drugs. For the most part, all **prescription** and over-the-counter drugs (OTCs) must be evaluated and approved by the FDA.

Drug manufacturers test new drugs for years before submitting them to the FDA. The agency then evaluates the data and decides whether a drug is safe for use. Even after a drug has been approved and is in use by the public, the FDA continues to monitor them. If the side effects of a drug are too dangerous, the FDA may even withdraw its approval.

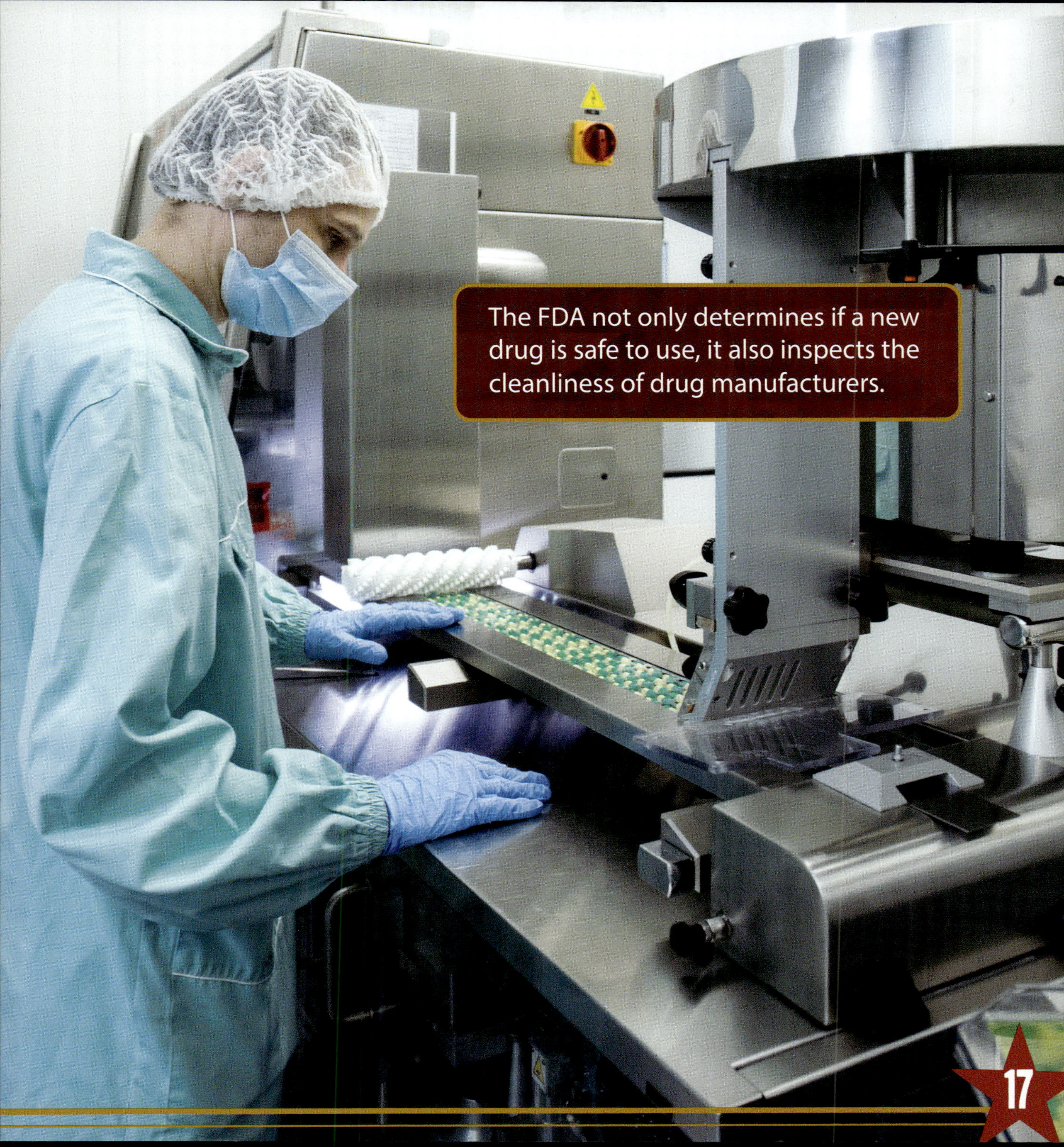

The FDA not only determines if a new drug is safe to use, it also inspects the cleanliness of drug manufacturers.

VACCINE APPROVAL

The FDA is also one step in the important process to approve new vaccines. Like medicinal drugs, vaccines undergo strict testing by manufacturers to make sure they're safe and effective. Then, the U.S. government gets involved. The FDA and another agency called the U.S. Centers for Disease Control and Prevention (CDC) must give approval.

During the COVID-19 pandemic in 2020, drug companies and the U.S. government put much effort into speeding up this process. The whole world was in need of a vaccine to limit the spread of the deadly virus. The COVID-19 vaccines set the record for fastest development and approval of a vaccine in U.S. history!

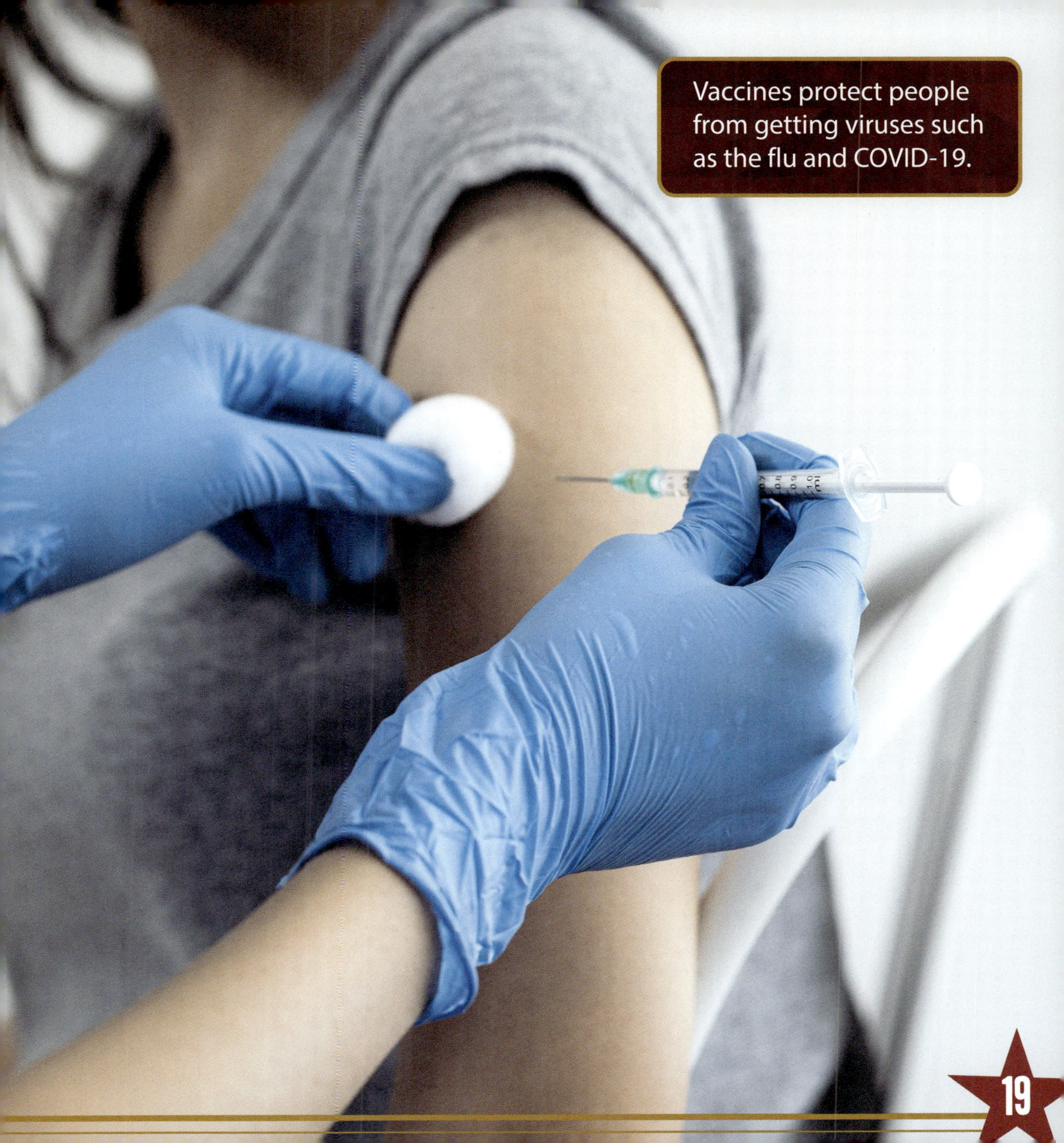

Vaccines protect people from getting viruses such as the flu and COVID-19.

A CAREER WITH THE FDA

There are many kinds of jobs within in the FDA. Since it's a health agency, the FDA is a perfect choice for someone interested in a scientific or medical career. There are nurses, pharmacists, biologists, chemists, doctors, veterinarians, and more working at the FDA!

If you're interested in learning about a career with the FDA, the agency offers many **internship** opportunities once you're a little older—for high school and college students. The FDA also offers training programs in many scientific fields. Whatever your age, it's never too early to start reading up on the FDA and public health!

Many FDA careers require a college degree in a scientific field.

GLOSSARY

cabinet: A committee of government officials who help the president run the country.

contaminant: A substance that is dangerous, dirty, or impure.

deceptive: Something that's misleading.

internship: An educational or training program that gives experience for a career.

mineral: A naturally occurring solid substance that is not of plant or animal origin. Sometimes sold as a supplement.

nutritious: Having to do with food that is healthy.

pathogen: A bacterium, virus, or other small organism that can cause illness.

pharmacy: A store where you can buy medicine and other health supplies.

prescription: An order for medicine or treatment given by a doctor.

symptom: Signs of disease or injury.

vitamin: A naturally occurring substance that is necessary for human growth. Sometimes sold as a supplement.

FOR MORE INFORMATION

BOOKS

Lee, Sally. *Food Safety*. Oxford, England: Raintree, 2021.

Morlock, Rachael. *Be Smart About Factory Foods*. Buffalo, NY: Cavendish Square Publishing, 2023.

Schwartz, Heather E. *Vaccine Breakthroughs*. Rochester, MN: Mayo Clinic Press Kids, 2024.

WEBSITES

Food and Drug Administration
www.fda.gov
Visit the official government website of the FDA.

World Health Organization: Foodborne Diseases
www.who.int/health-topics/foodborne-diseases#tab=tab_1
Learn more about foodborne illnesses around the world at the WHO website.

Publisher's note to educators and parents: Our editors have carefully reviewed these websites to ensure that they are suitable for students. Many websites change frequently, however, and we cannot guarantee that a site's future contents will continue to meet our high standards of quality and educational value. Be advised that students should be closely supervised whenever they access the internet.

INDEX